Origami

Origami

LINDA BARKER

SMITHMARK

Salamander Books Ltd., 1993
129-137 York Way,
London N7 9LG,
United Kingdom.

This edition published in 1993 by SMITHMARK Publishers Inc.,
16 East 32nd Street, New York, NY 10016.

ISBN 0 8317 1584 7

SMITHMARK books are available for bulk purchase for sales
promotion and premium use. For details write or telephone
the Manager of Special Sales, SMITHMARK Publishers Inc.,
16 East 32nd Street, New York, NY 10016. (212) 532-6600.

CREDITS

Author: Linda Barker

Managing Editor: Samantha Gray

Copy Editor: Alison Leach

Designer: Louise Bruce

Photographer: Graham Rae

Typeset by: BMD Graphics Ltd., Hemel Hempstead

Color Separation by: Scantrans Pte Ltd., Singapore

Printed in Singapore

CONTENTS

Introduction

6

Simple Designs

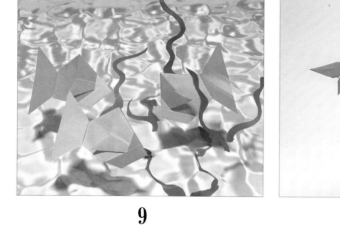

9

Intermediate Designs

33

Advanced Designs

49

Index
64

INTRODUCTION

This paper boat actually floats, giving children hours of fun.

Whether we realize it or not, most of us have practised the art of origami. Do you remember those dart-like airplanes which we used to throw around the classroom? It may surprise you to know that paper airplanes can become very sophisticated origami folds, far removed from the humble paper dart, with very serious competitions in which the best airplanes are judged with great solemnity. Those charming little umbrellas that decorate so many ice cream sundaes and cocktails are also forms of origami.

A friend of mine remembers being mesmerized as a child by the magical creation of a delightful flying crane that her grandfather made with the small square of gold paper from his cigarette pack. A tiny golden bird that could flap its tiny wings, what child could fail to be fascinated by such a simple but enchanting paper fold? There are several folds in this book that will delight younger children, such as the Samuri Hat that can be decorated for birthday parties, and the Windmill whose sails can catch the slightest breeze. With a little encouragement, children will be able to follow the illustrated step-by-step instructions and fold the designs themselves.

For those who like their origami to have a more practical function, origami folds that can be used in the kitchen or living-room and for children's parties are also included.

Origami, or or-i-gam'e (Japanese: oru, to fold; kami, paper), began with the invention of paper almost a thousand years ago. It has always had a wide appeal in the East but recently an increasing fascination in the art has developed in the West. Most importantly, it can be done anywhere at any time using just simple pieces of paper. Once you have mastered a few basic folds and creases, a whole world of creative paper-folding is there for you to discover.

This book is designed to introduce this surprisingly versatile art to the inexperienced paper-folder. The projects are devised so as to take you from the simplest folds to more complex designs. The easy-to-follow instructions will help you to achieve the best results for each project. Before starting to fold, there are a few golden rules that will prove helpful:

1

Always rest the paper you are folding on a hard level surface; as a beginner, do not attempt to fold the paper in the air.

2

Check that your paper is a true square or rectangle and a suitable size, depending on the project.

3

Check that the creases are aligned and press each crease firmly in one movement.

Various terms and symbols are used in origami and once you are familiar with these, you will be able to follow the illustrations in any book on the subject even if you do not understand the language! If you do become stuck, don't give up! Work back through the instructions to the point at which you feel most confident and try again slowly. As you work through the projects in this book, you will find that certain folds appear again and again; the more times you fold, the more proficient you become. Before you try to make any of the projects, practise the folds shown on page 8.

Use large squares of thick, colored paper to
make these wonderful gift boxes.
Tying them up with decorative ribbon adds a
perfect finishing touch.

ORIGAMI FOLDS

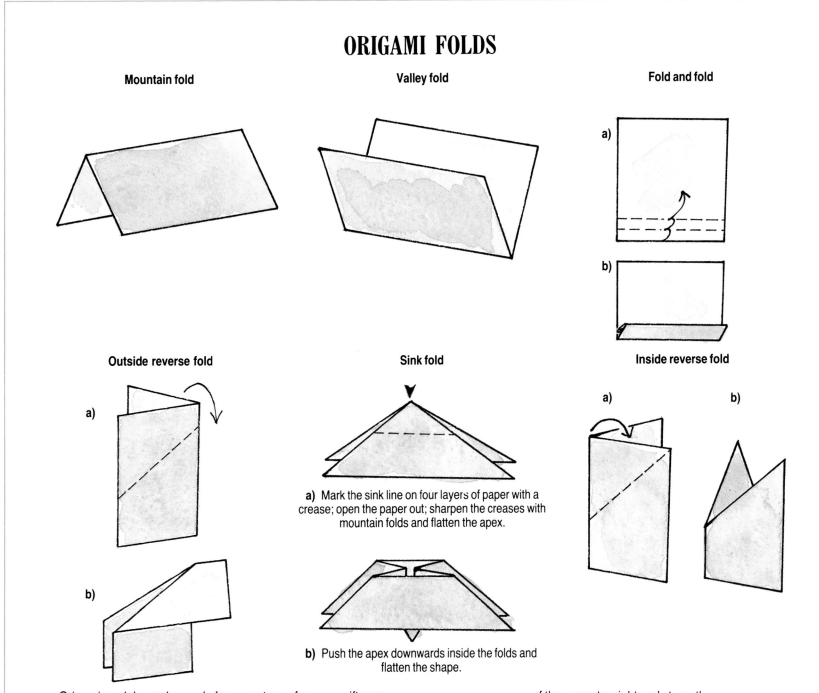

Mountain fold

Valley fold

Fold and fold

a)

b)

Outside reverse fold

a)

b)

Sink fold

a) Mark the sink line on four layers of paper with a crease; open the paper out; sharpen the creases with mountain folds and flatten the apex.

b) Push the apex downwards inside the folds and flatten the shape.

Inside reverse fold

a)

b)

Origami models can be made from any type of paper – gift wrap, newsprint or even pages of a magazine. However, there are special types of origami paper which are widely available in arts and crafts stores. These are cut to perfect squares of different sizes and can be used immediately. This special paper can be plain or patterned, is sometimes foil-backed and is often colored on both sides which can make the finished design most attractive. If you use paper that is colored on only one side, follow the photographs illustrating Step 1 of the different projects to determine which side of the paper should be uppermost.

It is undoubtedly worthwhile buying several packs of special origami paper to start your paper-folding; you are then certain that the paper is of the correct weight and strength.

Choose the paper with a color and pattern most suited to your design. For example, the pretty Spanish Box (page 13) would benefit from a paper that is patterned on one side and plain on the other to show off its attractive accordion-folded edges, whereas the delicate Flying Crane (page 48) needs plain paper so that you can see the folded detail in its wings clearly.

As you become more experienced in the art of origami, you will become adept at choosing the right paper for a particular design from the very beautiful papers which are available, but initially just enjoy the folding. Until you understand how to make all the folds, practise with scraps of cheap paper.

CHAPTER ONE

SIMPLE DESIGNS

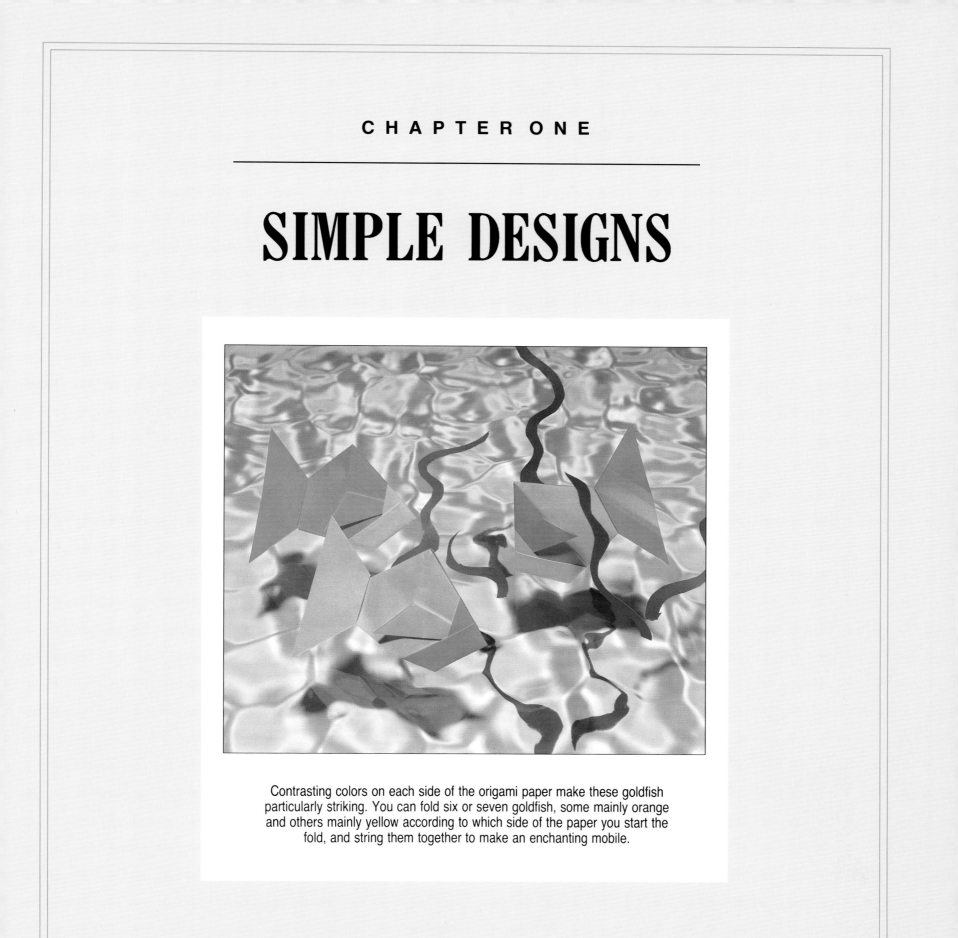

Contrasting colors on each side of the origami paper make these goldfish particularly striking. You can fold six or seven goldfish, some mainly orange and others mainly yellow according to which side of the paper you start the fold, and string them together to make an enchanting mobile.

Windmill

1 Crease the vertical center line of the paper and open it out. Valley fold the left- and right-hand edges to meet at the center. Fold the top and bottom edges inwards so that they meet at the center and form a square.

2 Fold the free corners of the top flap to meet at the center top and the free corners of the bottom flap to meet at the center bottom. Unfold. Pull out the inner layer under the top flap and pull both points outwards. Repeat with the bottom flap.

3 Fold the top right-hand corner flap upwards as shown, and fold the bottom left-hand corner flap downwards to form the windmill. Pin the windmill onto a stick. It will whirl around and around in the slightest breeze.

Coaster

1 Fold the paper as for the Windmill (opposite) until you have completed Step 2. Lift the top left-hand fold vertically and squash it until it is completely flat. Repeat with the other three folds to form a square as shown in Step 2.

2 Each squashed fold has two inner edges. Make tiny triangular-shaped valley folds on each of these edges as shown.

3 Keeping your right thumb on the center, lift each tiny fold vertically and open each one by pressing the outer tip flat to form a triangle as shown.

Salt Cellar

1 Fold the opposite edges of a square of paper together in turn, crease and then open out. Turn the paper over and fold across the diagonals, then open out. Turn the paper over again and fold all four corners into the center to form a square as shown.

2 Turn the paper over and again fold each corner into the center to form a smaller square. Turn the paper over again and fold across the diagonals. Open this last fold out.

3 Squash two opposite corners inwards, pinch the top and pull out the four flaps carefully. Fill the four compartments with salt. This traditional paper fold is often used by children to conceal fortunes or forfeits.

Spanish Box

1 This pretty box can hold candy or small pieces of jewelery. Crease the diagonal lines across the center of the paper and fold the four corners inwards to meet at the center to form a square.

2 Turn the paper over and fold the four corners inwards to meet at the center to form a smaller square. Valley fold the four central points so that they extend just beyond the outer edges of the square, as shown.

3 Turn the paper over and valley fold each of the four flaps in half across the diagonal. Pleat these small flaps very carefully, by making six tiny equal-sized valley and mountain folds. Push your thumb into each corner and press the two sides together to make the box.

The Crown

1 Fold the paper as for the G I Hat (p28) until you have completed Step 4. Fold in the bottom corners across the diagonal; turn the paper over and repeat this step.

2 Fold up the top layer of the 'new' corner to the center of the top edge. Turn the paper over and repeat with the remaining layer.

3 Open out the bottom edge and press the two colored points together until you have made a crown shape. To make the crown more festive, stick brightly colored gems or beads on the points or paint them in different colors.

Flower Decorations

1 Fold the paper as for the Coaster (p11) until you have completed Step 1. Each square fold has two inner edges. Make small triangular-shaped valley folds on each of these edges as shown.

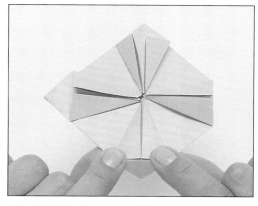

2 Fold the four corners backwards as shown. To enhance the flower shape, stick a small circle of colored paper in the center. Lift each small fold vertically and open each one by pressing the outer tip flat to form a triangle.

3 Make six of these flower shapes and stick them together at the corners to form a very attractive decoration that could be suspended from the ceiling. Shiny papers are particularly effective for making this design.

Samurai Hat

1 Fold the paper across the diagonal to form a triangle. Then fold down the right- and left-hand points so that they meet at the bottom point. Valley fold the open points upwards until they meet the top point.

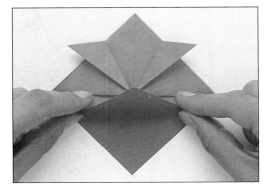

2 Fold the two top points backwards to form tiny wings on the left and right as shown. Fold the top layer of the lower flap up so that the tip meets the base point of the wings.

3 Fold the base of the flap upwards as shown. Fold the remaining lower flap underneath and open out the base of the hat. This traditional origami fold is sometimes called a Japanese helmet. It provides a useful base from which other designs can be made.

Goldfish

1 Start with a completed Samurai Hat (opposite). With the wings facing you, push the two sides of the hat together as shown. Using a pair of scissors, cut along the fold on the lower right-hand edge, to about three-quarters of the length. Repeat on the left-hand edge.

2 Pinch the center of the bottom front of the hat with one hand and with the other hand carefully open up the shape that will form the tail of the goldfish.

3 Fold a small section of the lower edge inwards as shown. Repeat this step on the other side. Although the paper must not be cut in making pure origami folds, a small cut is needed to make the tail. String six or seven goldfish together to make a mobile.

Cup

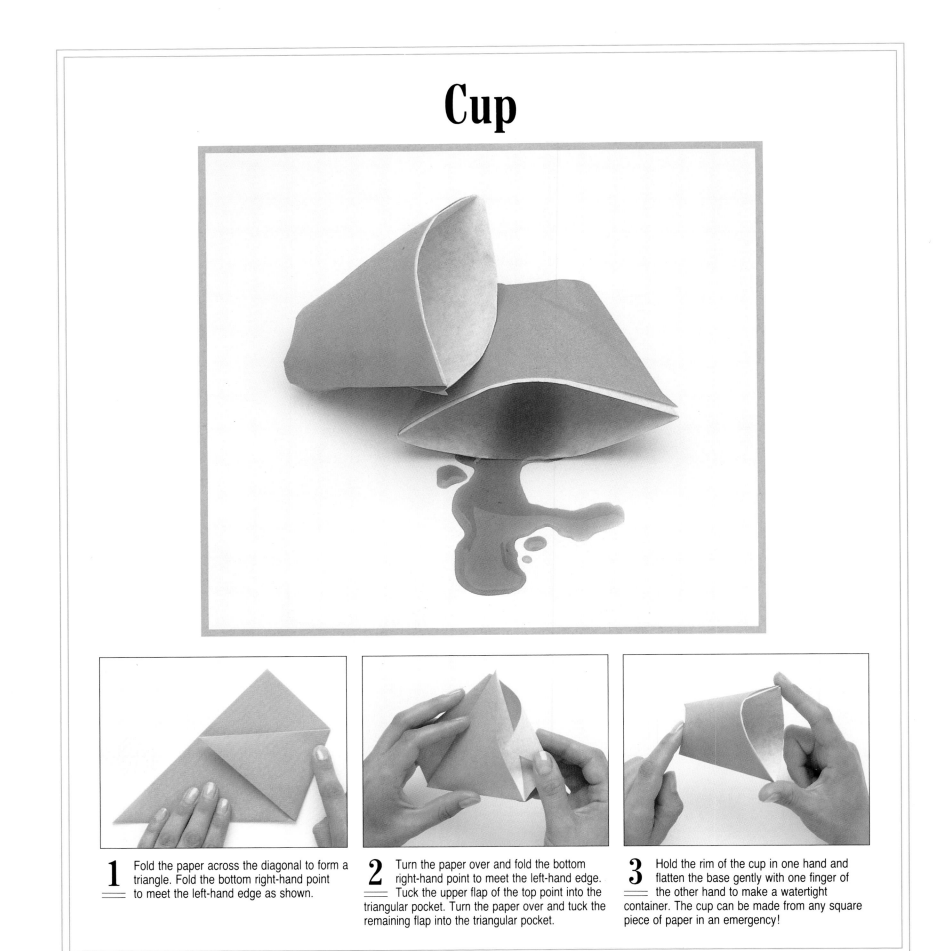

1 Fold the paper across the diagonal to form a triangle. Fold the bottom right-hand point to meet the left-hand edge as shown.

2 Turn the paper over and fold the bottom right-hand point to meet the left-hand edge. Tuck the upper flap of the top point into the triangular pocket. Turn the paper over and tuck the remaining flap into the triangular pocket.

3 Hold the rim of the cup in one hand and flatten the base gently with one finger of the other hand to make a watertight container. The cup can be made from any square piece of paper in an emergency!

Yakko-San

1 Complete Step 1 of the Salt Cellar (p12); then turn the paper over and again fold each corner into the center to form a smaller square. Fold the four corners into the center once more, pressing the folds firmly.

2 Turn the paper over and pre-crease across the diagonals of three of the small squares as shown.

3 Separate the free edges of these three squares in the center and squash fold as shown. Paint the features of a face on the remaining square. Yakko-San is the name of a traditional Japanese clown.

Booklet

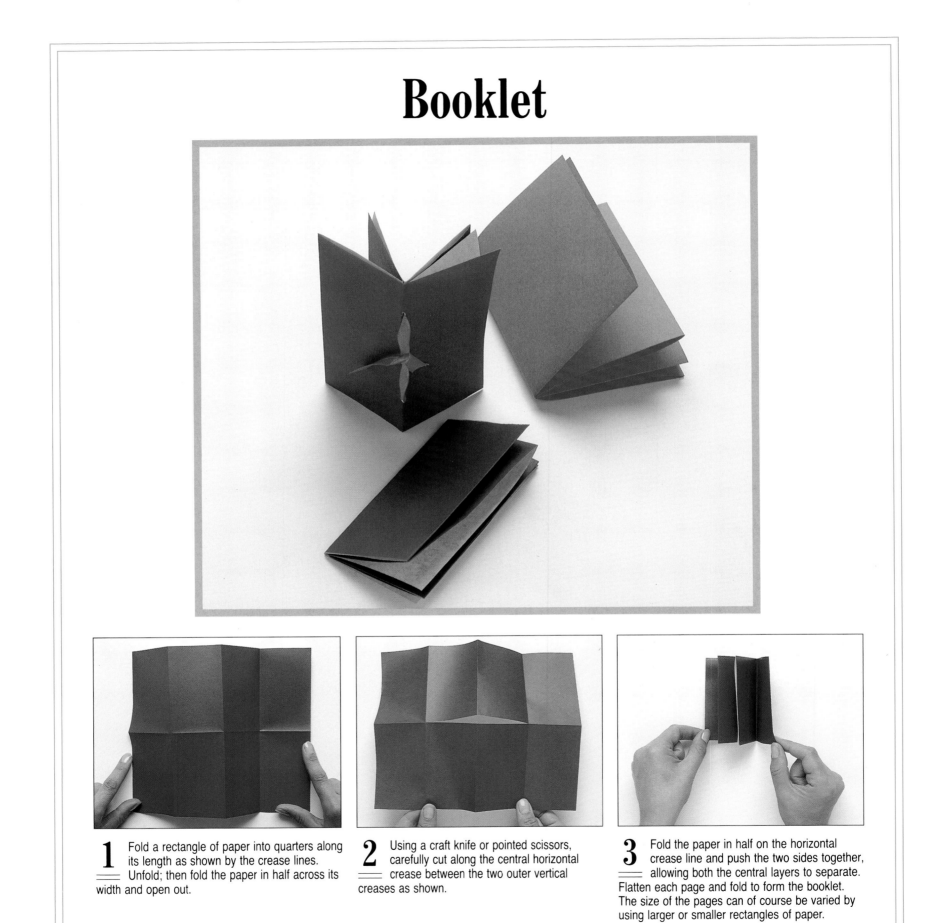

1 Fold a rectangle of paper into quarters along its length as shown by the crease lines. Unfold; then fold the paper in half across its width and open out.

2 Using a craft knife or pointed scissors, carefully cut along the central horizontal crease between the two outer vertical creases as shown.

3 Fold the paper in half on the horizontal crease line and push the two sides together, allowing both the central layers to separate. Flatten each page and fold to form the booklet. The size of the pages can of course be varied by using larger or smaller rectangles of paper.

Four- or Eight-pointed Star

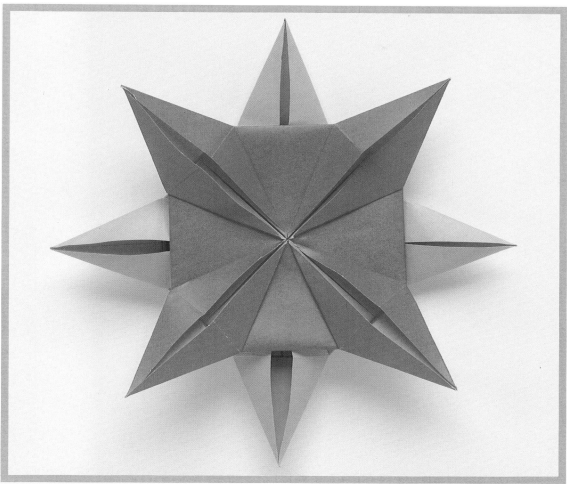

1 This star shows the technique of making a petal fold, often used in origami. Start with the shape made after completing Step 1 of the Flower Decorations (p15). Mountain fold the four corners underneath.

2 Open out the folded inner edges of one flap and lift up the pointed tip until its edges meet in the center to form a diamond shape which is the basis of a petal fold. Repeat this step with the remaining flaps and press the design flat to make a four-pointed star.

3 To create an eight-pointed star, place two of the four-pointed stars together, crosswise, back to back, and fold the four tiny triangles of one star around the front of the other. This looks very effective if the stars are made from different colored paper but are identical in size.

Corner Fastener

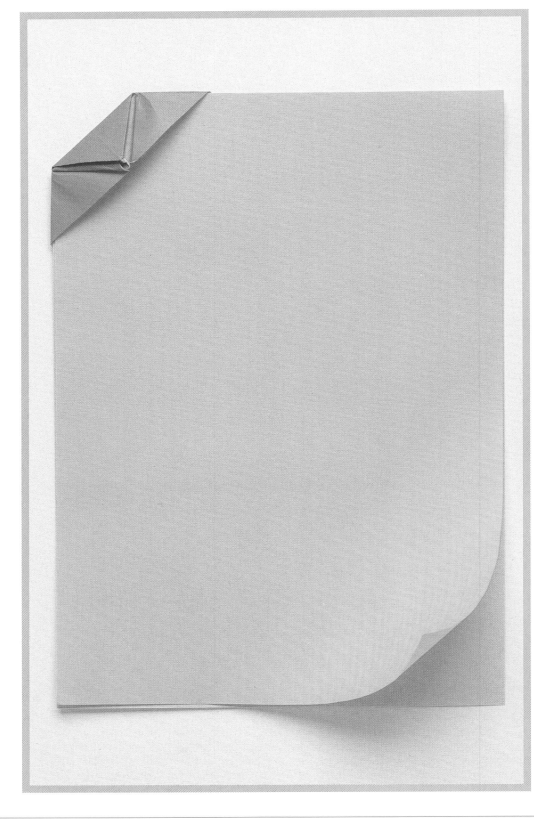

1 Fold the opposite edges of a square of paper together in turn, crease and then open out. Fold the paper across each diagonal, then open out. Push the centers of two sides of the square together as shown until they form a triangle.

2 Place the sheets of paper as far as possible into the lower pocket. Fold the two opposite corners of the top flap to the center of the diagonal edge.

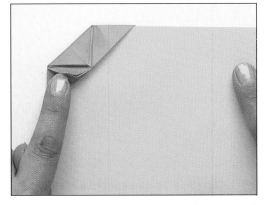

3 Fold the top point over to meet the center of the diagonal edge. Tuck the two tiny triangular flaps up inside the adjacent pockets to complete.

Seed Envelope

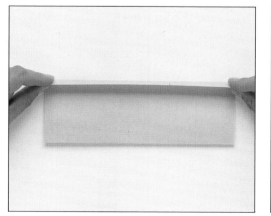

1 You will need a rectangle of paper, not a square, to make this clever design which was first folded by a schoolgirl. Fold up one of the long edges to within 1 inch of the other long edge. Fold the top flap over and over once more; then turn the paper over.

2 Fold the top left- and right-hand corners inwards to meet the lower edge as shown.

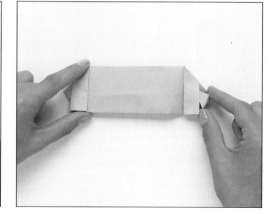

3 Fold the bottom left- and right-hand points inwards and tuck them under the side flaps to complete the envelope. Open up one end to fill or empty. It resembles an old-fashioned seed envelope but it can also be used to hold a variety of tiny items.

Butterfly

1 Start with the base formed at the end of Step 2 of the Windmill (p10). Turn the base over and valley fold in half from the top to the bottom, pressing the fold firmly.

2 Valley fold the top layer of the top left- and right-hand points downwards until they meet and form a triangle.

3 Position the shape as shown and make a tiny valley fold on the two sides where indicated in the photograph.

4 Turn the shape over and valley fold in half from the top to the bottom, pressing the fold firmly.

5 Valley fold the corner of the bottom right-hand flap over to the left on a slight slant as shown.

6 Open the shape and fold the middle point over and then back again so it stands vertical. If you press down carefully on the upright point of the butterfly, it will gently flutter its wings.

Shallow Box

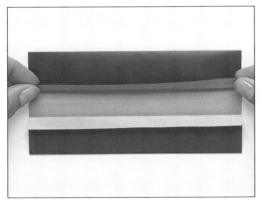

1 To make a functional leak-proof box, you can use waterproof paper or foil. Pre-crease the paper by valley folding it in half from left to right and then opening it out. Fold the two outer edges to this crease. Turn back narrow hems of equal width on both these edges.

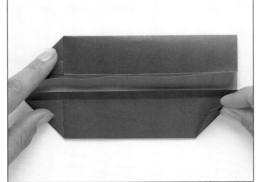

2 Unfold the hems. Fold the four corners inwards to touch the creases made by the hems in Step 1.

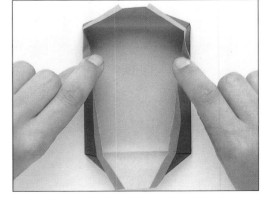

3 Fold both flaps inwards and crease the edges to form a rectangle. Re-fold the two hems. Push your fingers into the four corners and lift up the sides to form the box. Squeeze the corners to make them square.

Box on Legs

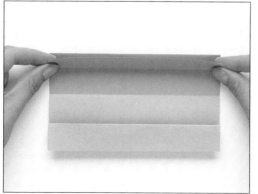

1 Pre-crease the paper by valley folding it in half from left to right and then opening it out. Fold the two outer edges to the center crease. Turn back wide hems of equal width on both these edges so that the two flaps extend beyond the existing edges. Unfold the hems.

2 Fold the four corners inwards to touch the creases made by the hems. Note how much smaller the resulting triangles are than those in the Shallow Box (opposite).

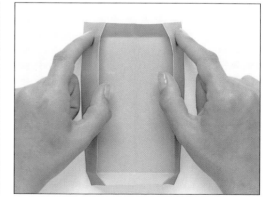

3 Turn both flaps inwards and crease the edges to form a rectangle. Re-fold the two hems. Push your fingers into the four corners and lift up the sides to form the box. Squeeze the corners to make them square.

G I Hat

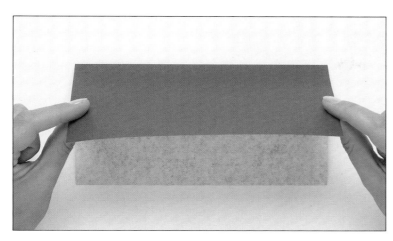

1 Use medium- to heavy-weight paper, about 15-20 inch square, to make a hat that can be worn at a children's party, and choose a color that co-ordinates with the disposable cups and plates. Valley fold the paper in half.

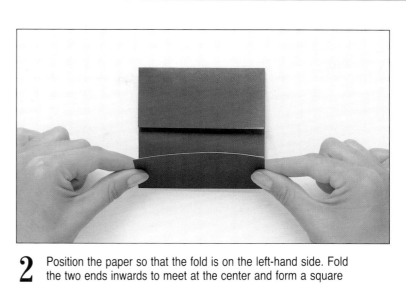

2 Position the paper so that the fold is on the left-hand side. Fold the two ends inwards to meet at the center and form a square as shown; then unfold.

3 Slip the forefinger of your right hand under the top fold to open the corner; then squash the left-hand fold open. Repeat with the bottom fold so that the edges meet in the center as shown.

4 Fold the top and bottom flaps underneath to form a square. Then turn the paper so that the crease is on the top.

5 Fold the top layer of the bottom half upwards three times. Turn the paper over and fold the remaining layer in the same way.

6 Push your thumbs into the two corners and slightly squash down the middle of the hat to open it and make the characteristic dip.

Preliminary Base

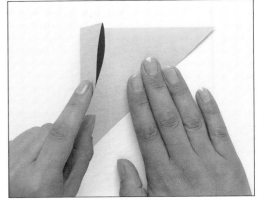

1 Valley fold a square of paper in half across the diagonal to form a triangle. Then valley fold in half again from left to right as shown.

2 Holding the lower flap down with one hand, lift the upper flap with the other hand and squash fold, as shown, to open it out.

3 Turn the paper over and repeat the previous step on this side to form a square. This is one of the most important bases in origami. It is used to create a number of the models included in the next chapter.

Bird Base

1 Start by completing the Preliminary Base (opposite) and position the square with the open points nearest you. Fold the top layers of the right- and left-hand sides inwards to meet the center crease and form a point at the base. Turn the paper over and repeat this step on this side.

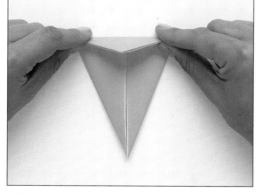

2 Fold the top point downwards over the horizontal edges as shown.

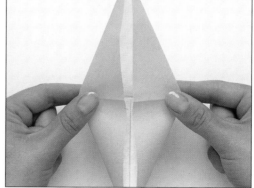

3 Pick up the corners as shown to open out the inner flaps and petal fold (see Four- or Eight-pointed Star, p21) the bottom point upwards. Turn the shape over and repeat this step to complete the base. This is probably the base that is most used, so it is important to perfect your folding of it.

Simple Boat

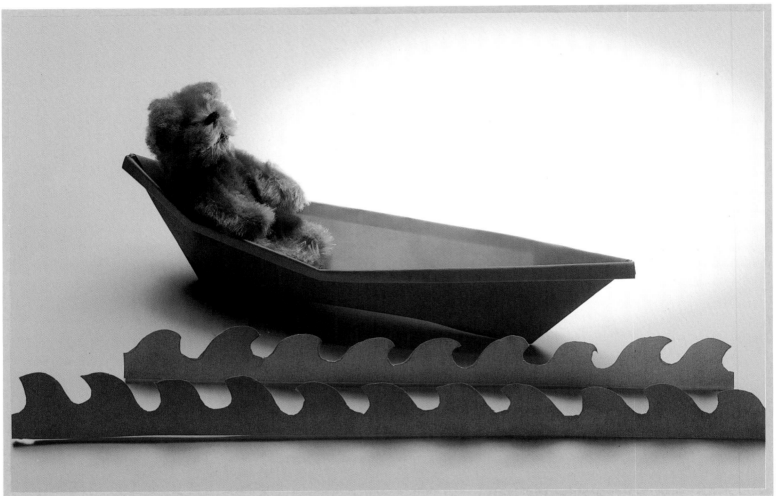

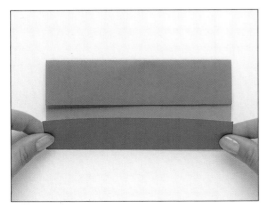

1 Crease the horizontal center line of the paper, then open out. Fold the two edges inwards to meet the center crease line. Fold in half lengthwise.

2 Position the paper so that the open side is on the right. Fold the top and bottom left-hand corners inwards on the diagonal, leaving a narrow edge as shown.

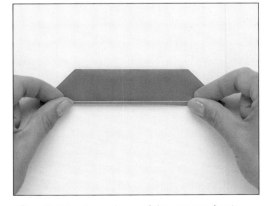

3 Fold back one layer of the upper edge to form a hem and fold over once again. Turn the paper over and repeat on this side. Crease along the base to flatten the bottom of the boat. Open out to form a boat that can float.

CHAPTER TWO

INTERMEDIATE DESIGNS

Beautiful, folded paper flowers have long been part of Japanese culture and the elegantly shaped iris is an especially popular fold. You can make paper irises in a variety of colors to decorate your home – attach the flowers to wire 'stems' and cut out sword-shaped leaves for an authentic touch.

Bracelet

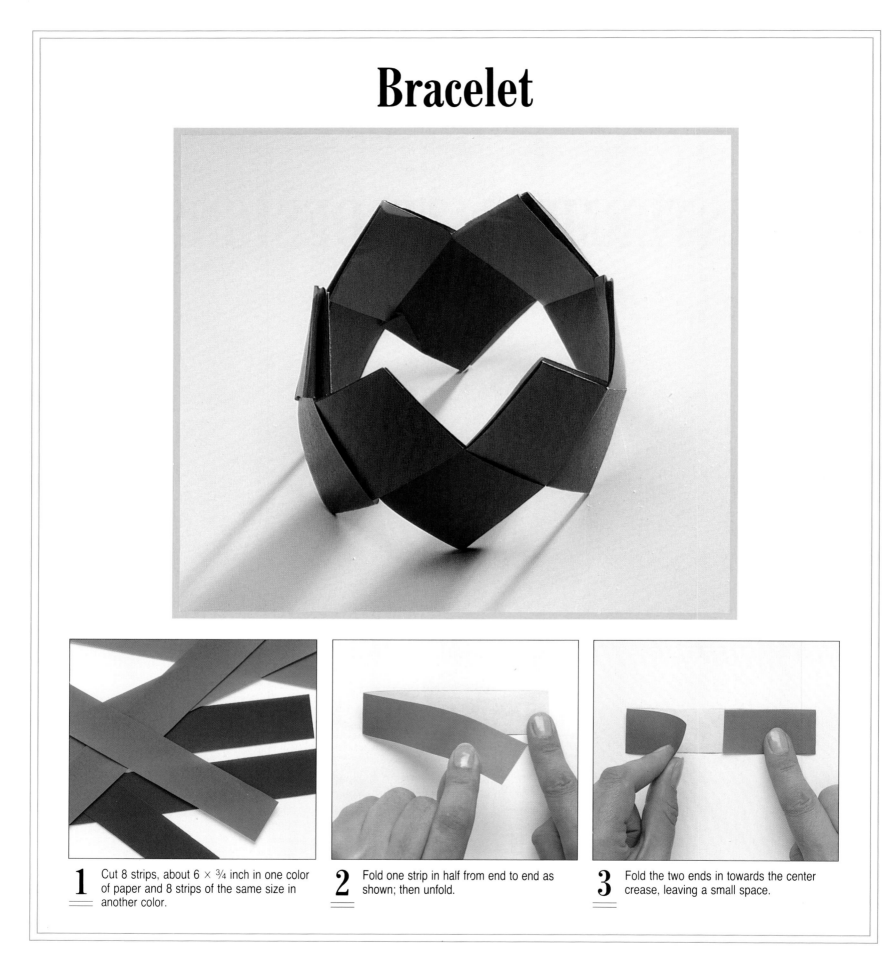

1 Cut 8 strips, about 6 × ¾ inch in one color of paper and 8 strips of the same size in another color.

2 Fold one strip in half from end to end as shown; then unfold.

3 Fold the two ends in towards the center crease, leaving a small space.

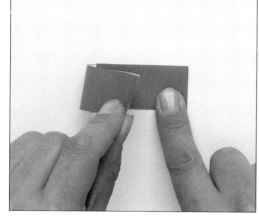

4 Fold this shape in half from end to end.

5 Repeat Steps 2-4 with all the strips. Slide a strip of one color inside the layers of another strip of the other color to lock together and form an L-shape.

6 Slide in the third strip, in the same color as the second strip, in the same way, forming a zigzag shape as shown.

7 Slide in a fourth strip, in the same color as the first strip, in the same way.

8 Repeat this procedure, alternating the colors, until only one strip is left.

9 Unfold the last creases in the remaining strip so that it is only folded in half from end to end.

10 Slide this longer strip inside the layers of the previous one.

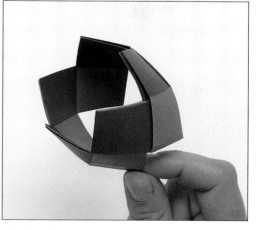

11 Tuck the loose ends of the last strip inside the other end of the bracelet.

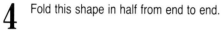

12 The bracelet is now securely fastened. The length can be adjusted by using a larger or smaller number of strips.

Iris

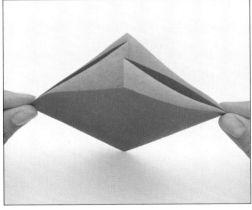

1 Start with the Preliminary Base (p30) and position the square as shown with the open points upwards.

2 Fold the upper right- and left-hand flaps inwards until the edges meet in the center; then unfold to reveal the crease lines.

3 Holding the left-hand flap down with one finger, open the right-hand flap and make a petal fold (see Four- or Eight-pointed Star, p21) to the left as shown, pressing it flat.

4 Fold the shape across the central horizontal line to make a sharp crease; then unfold.

5 Fold the upper right- and left-hand edges of the petal fold inwards until they meet in the center. Unfold.

6 Put a finger into the petal fold and pull down the center of the horizontal edge until it forms a point.

7 Turn the paper over and repeat Steps 2-6. Then repeat Steps 2-6 on the remaining two sides, each time folding the preceding diamond shape underneath.

8 Fold the tiny central pointed flap upwards. Repeat this step, turning over the layers carefully to find each of the three similar concealed flaps.

9 Fold the top left-hand flap across to meet the right-hand one. Turn the shape over and repeat this step.

10 Fold the front lower left- and right-hand edges inwards to meet in the center. Repeat this step, turning over the layers carefully to find the three similar concealed flaps.

11 Fold down the top point and repeat this step with the remaining three points.

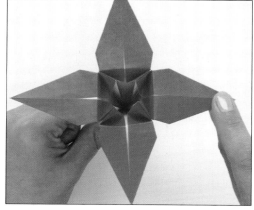

12 Fold the flaps at right angles to complete the flower.

Rooster

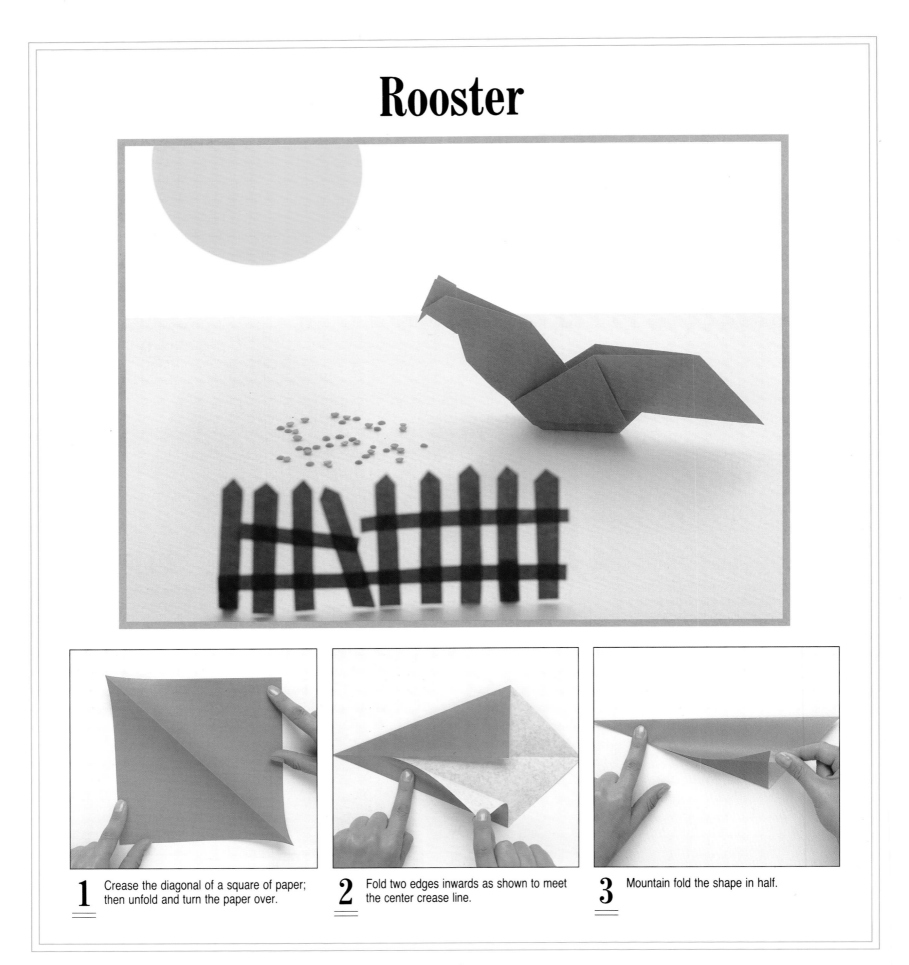

1 Crease the diagonal of a square of paper; then unfold and turn the paper over.

2 Fold two edges inwards as shown to meet the center crease line.

3 Mountain fold the shape in half.

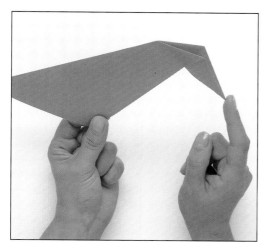

4 Inside reverse fold (see diagram, p8) the narrow point to form the neck.

5 Inside reverse fold the larger section to make the shape shown.

6 Fold down the front flap at the point shown, creasing into the corner. Unfold and repeat on the reverse side.

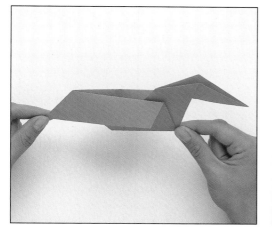

7 Open the shape out and mountain fold it across the crease lines you made in Step 6.

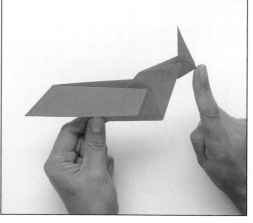

8 Inside reverse fold the neck section back again at the point shown.

9 Once again inside reverse fold a smaller section forwards at the point shown to complete the head.

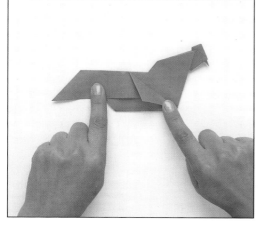

10 Fold down the flap that will form the wing. Turn the shape over and repeat this step on the reverse side.

11 Pull the triangular flap that lies beneath the wing forwards. Turn the shape over and repeat this step.

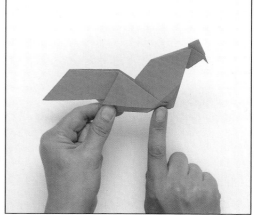

12 Mountain fold the lower right-hand corner backwards to shape the body. Turn the shape over and repeat this step.

Star-shaped Box

1 Start with the Preliminary Base (p30). Position the square with the open points to the top. Fold the left- and right-hand edges of the top layer inwards to meet at the center crease as shown.

2 Make two triangular creases in the flaps as shown.

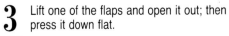

3 Lift one of the flaps and open it out; then press it down flat.

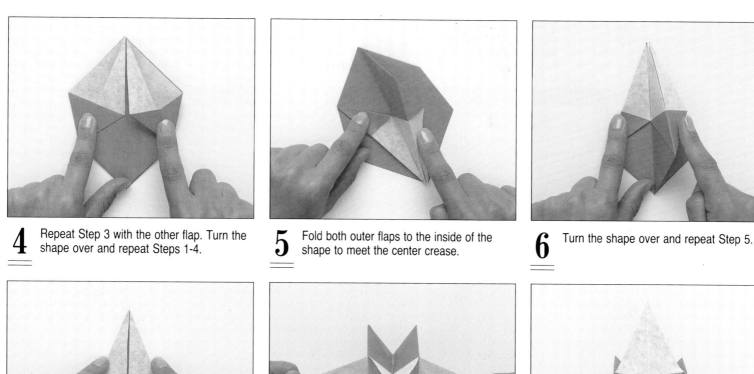

4 Repeat Step 3 with the other flap. Turn the shape over and repeat Steps 1-4.

5 Fold both outer flaps to the inside of the shape to meet the center crease.

6 Turn the shape over and repeat Step 5.

7 Fold the bottom point upwards to make a horizontal crease. Unfold. Turn the shape over and repeat this step.

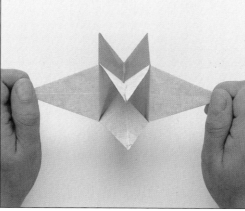

8 Holding two facing points, pull these apart gently, slowly opening the box.

9 Make sharp creases on the four top edges of the box to form the projecting triangles.

10 Push out the square base of the box with a finger as shown.

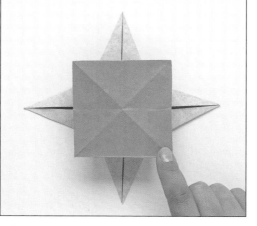

11 Turn the box over and make sharp creases along the edges of the base.

12 Turn the finished box over and fill with candy or small cookies. This box looks most attractive if you use paper that is plain on one side and patterned on the other. The pattern should be folded on the inside.

Cubic Gift Box

1 Use a slightly thicker paper than the usual origami paper to make this box. Mountain fold the vertical and horizontal center lines as shown; then unfold the square.

2 Turn the paper over and valley fold the four corners to meet in the center.

3 Fold the square vertically and horizontally into thirds. Unfold the paper to reveal the creases of the resulting nine squares.

4 Unfold the top and bottom triangular flaps.

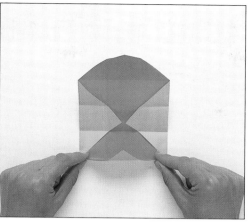

5 Re-crease the existing creases by valley folding each of them.

6 Hold the right-hand triangular flap as shown and lift this upwards around the central square to form one side of the box.

7 Holding the right-hand flap in position with one hand, repeat Step 6 with the left-hand triangular flap. Some dexterity is needed as the box seems to be collapsing.

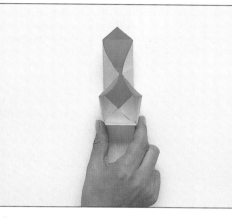

8 Fold the bottom triangular flap over the rim of the box, using the crease lines as a guide, until the point meets the center of the base of the box.

9 Repeat Step 8 with the remaining flap to complete the box.

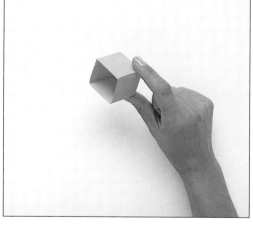

10 Flatten all the edges to make the shape really crisp.

11 Using a slightly larger piece of paper in a contrasting color, make another box in the same way.

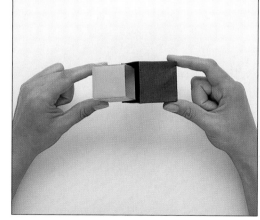

12 Push the smaller box inside the larger one; it should fit tightly. If liked, use a slightly larger square of paper to make the same shape to act as a lid.

Picture Frame

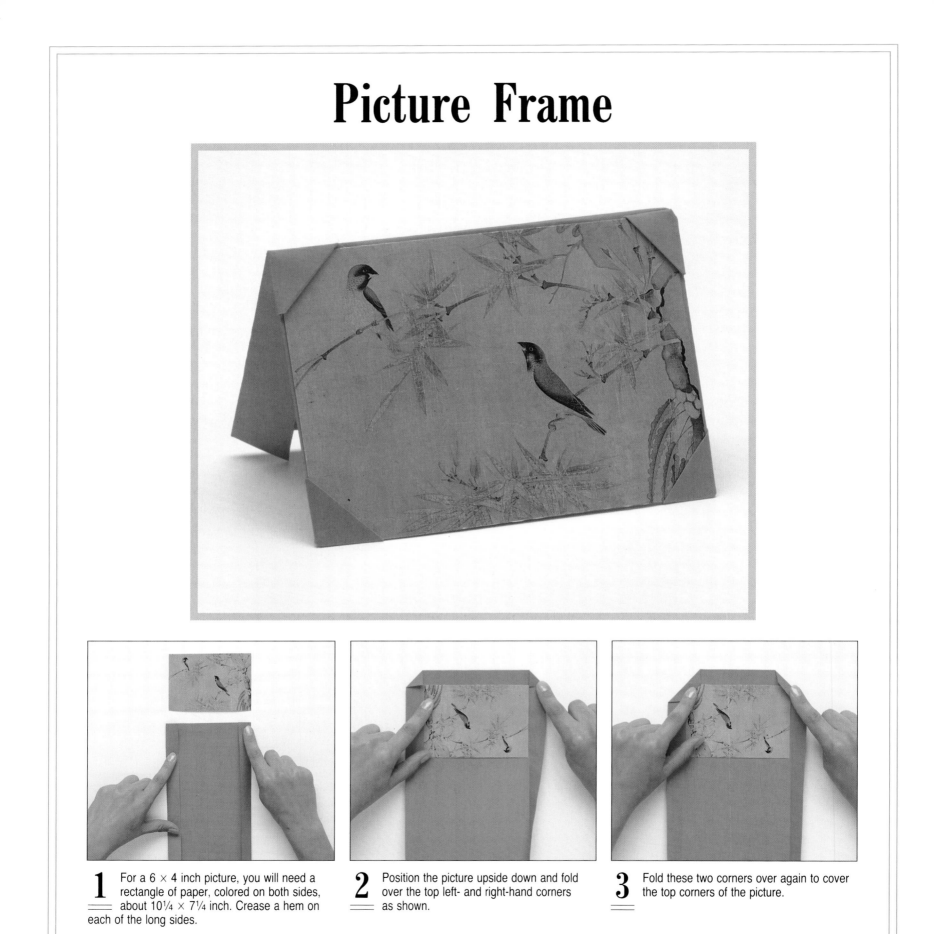

1 For a 6 × 4 inch picture, you will need a rectangle of paper, colored on both sides, about 10¼ × 7¼ inch. Crease a hem on each of the long sides.

2 Position the picture upside down and fold over the top left- and right-hand corners as shown.

3 Fold these two corners over again to cover the top corners of the picture.

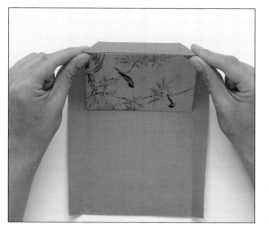

4 Fold the top edge backwards to align with the top edge of the picture.

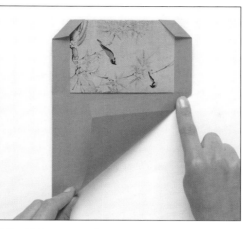

5 Make a small diagonal crease in the hem on the right-hand edge just below the picture.

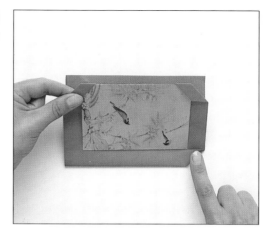

6 Fold the lower section of the paper backwards along an imaginary line crossing the tiny diagonal crease made in Step 5.

7 Fold the bottom corners to form tiny triangles, as in Step 2.

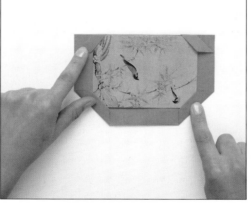

8 Fold these corners over once again to cover the lower edge of the picture.

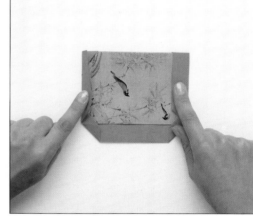

9 Fold the two sides backwards; then unfold. Fold the sides forwards, then unfold.

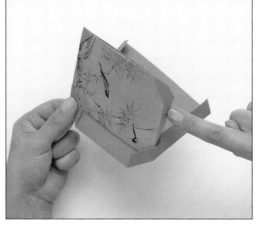

10 Carefully reverse fold (see diagram, p8) these edges to the inside, keeping the back section free.

11 Repeat Step 10 with the bottom edge. This last fold may be easier if you lift out the bottom edge of the picture.

12 Turn over to see the completed frame. Open out the back section to form a support for the frame. The folded edges on the sides help to hold it in position.

Cygnet

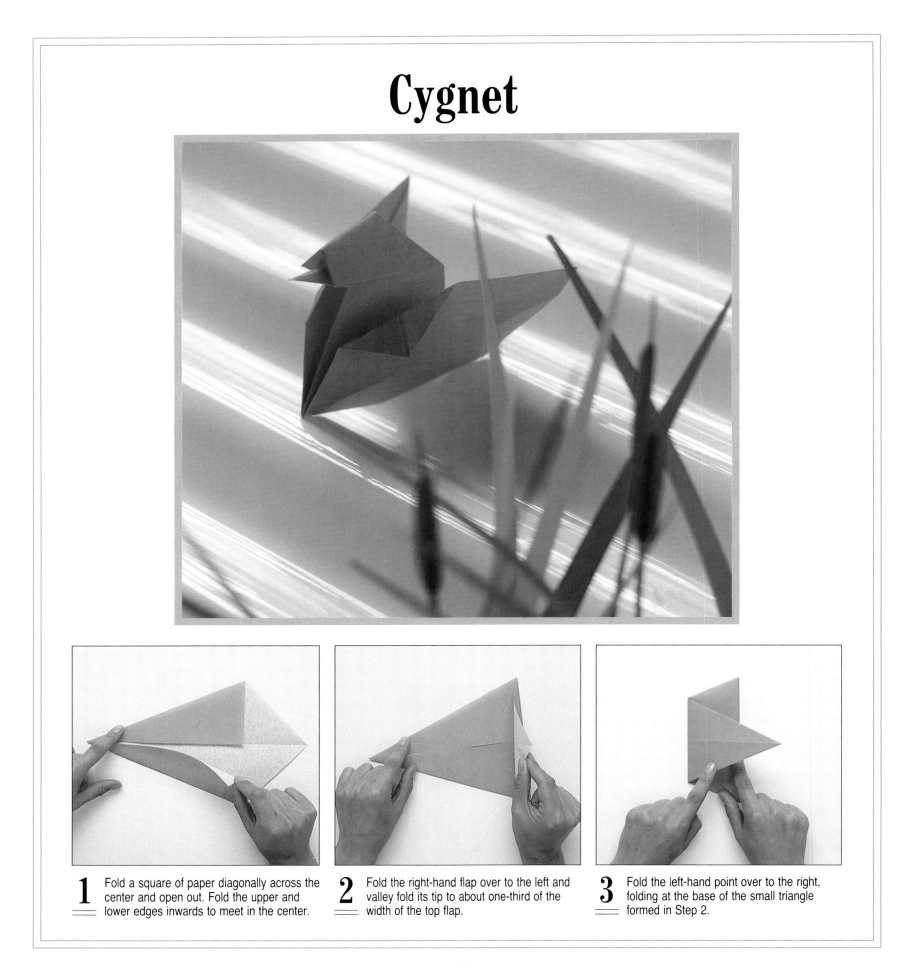

1 Fold a square of paper diagonally across the center and open out. Fold the upper and lower edges inwards to meet in the center.

2 Fold the right-hand flap over to the left and valley fold its tip to about one-third of the width of the top flap.

3 Fold the left-hand point over to the right, folding at the base of the small triangle formed in Step 2.

4 Valley fold the left-hand top and bottom sections inwards so that their edges meet the central horizontal line as shown.

5 Pick up the shape and open it by pushing a finger into the pocket underneath.

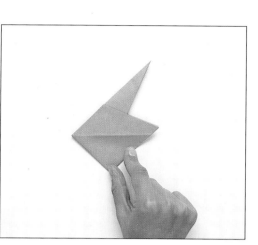

6 Squash the shape so it folds in half.

7 Fold down the top point of the diamond shape horizontally as shown. Turn the shape over and repeat this step.

8 Outside reverse fold (see diagram, p8) the head section and press flat.

9 Valley fold a small triangle along the base of the shape, unfold and inside reverse fold (see diagram, p8) the triangle.

10 Make a valley fold near the tip of the beak and a mountain fold a little nearer towards the head.

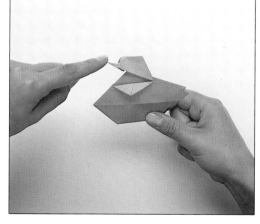

11 Open the head slightly and fold the beak inwards on the first fold.

12 Fold the beak outwards on the second fold. Press flat to complete the cygnet.

Flying Crane

1 Start with the completed Bird Base (p31). Fold the top left-hand triangle over to meet the top right-hand one. Turn the paper over and repeat this step on this side.

2 Inside reverse fold (see diagram, p8) the bottom point upwards to meet the top point. Turn the paper over and repeat this step on this side. Pull the right- and left-hand inner points out to the sides and fold to hold them in position.

3 Inside reverse fold the right-hand point to form the bird's head.

CHAPTER THREE

ADVANCED DESIGNS

One of the most impressive and delightful of all origami creatures, this prancing antelope has fine details including a distinctive pair of horns and a tail. Its stunning shape makes it a decorative ornament, or you could even use it as an extra-special greeting card.

Mouse

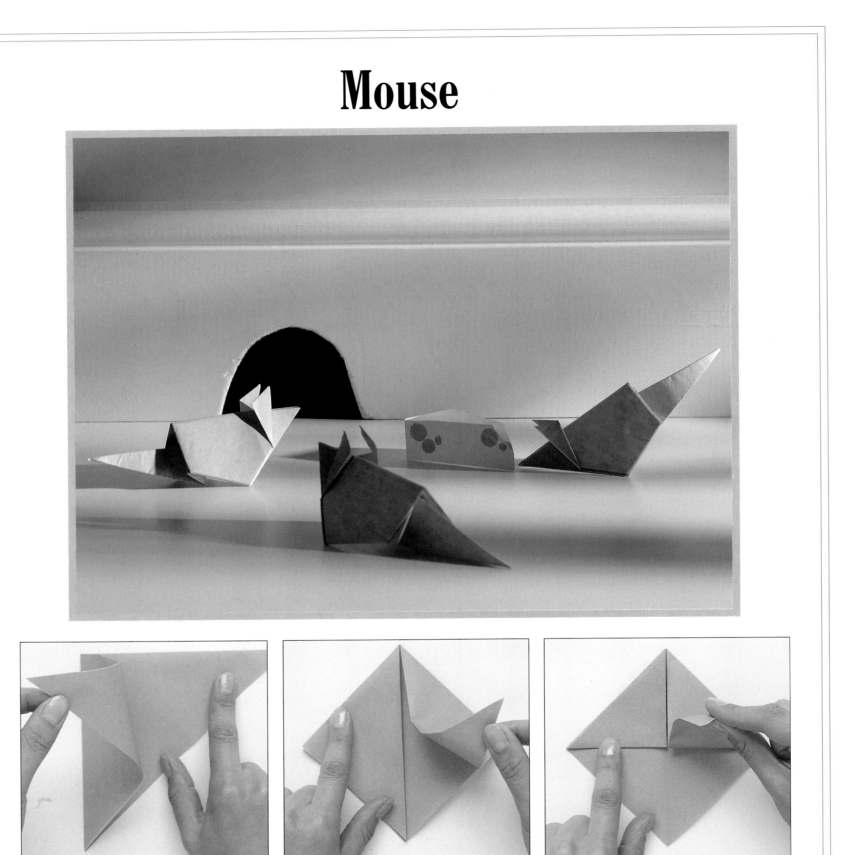

1 Fold a square of paper in half across the diagonal. Crease the center line by folding the shape in half again; then unfold.

2 Fold two opposite corners downwards to meet in the center.

3 Fold these two corners upwards to meet the top point, folding across their center.

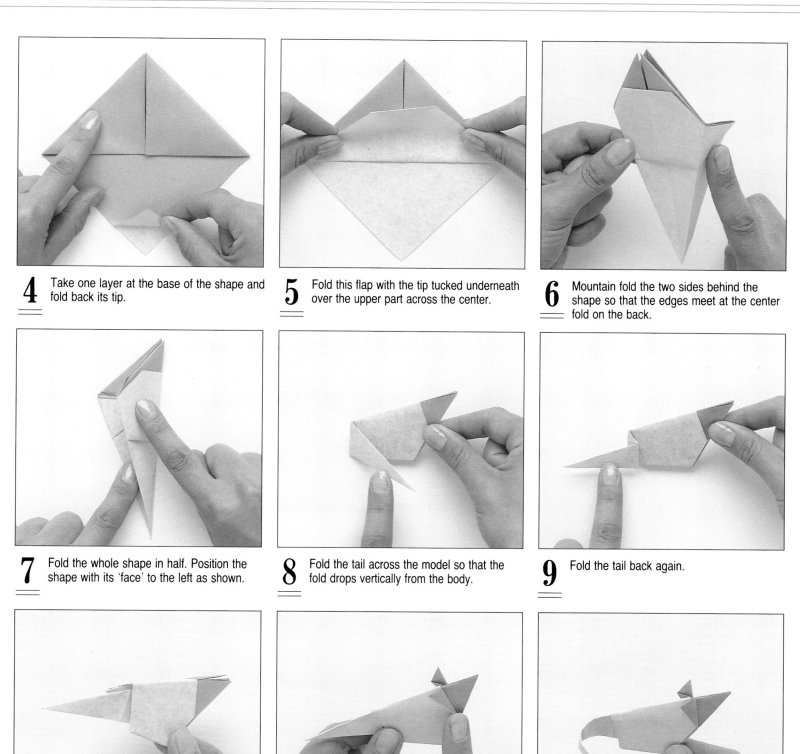

4 Take one layer at the base of the shape and fold back its tip.

5 Fold this flap with the tip tucked underneath over the upper part across the center.

6 Mountain fold the two sides behind the shape so that the edges meet at the center fold on the back.

7 Fold the whole shape in half. Position the shape with its 'face' to the left as shown.

8 Fold the tail across the model so that the fold drops vertically from the body.

9 Fold the tail back again.

10 Tuck the tail section inside the body, creasing the point where the tail is neatly concealed.

11 Fold back the 'ears' as far as they will go; then fold the same point back again so that the ears stand up in sharp points.

12 Curl the tail section slightly.

Swan

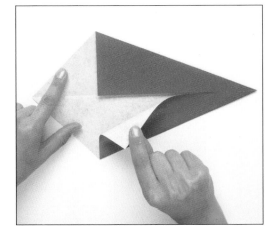

1 Crease a diagonal line across the center of the paper and position the square as shown. Fold in two adjacent edges to meet in the center on the crease line.

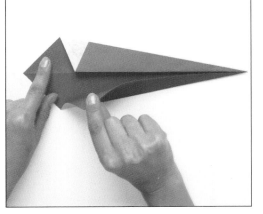

2 Turn the paper over and bring the folded edges inwards to meet in the center.

3 Fold the narrow right-hand point to the left to meet the other point; then fold the tip of the narrow point back as shown.

4 Taking great care, mountain fold the whole shape in half. Rotate the shape so it is seen in profile.

5 Lift up the triangular shape that will form the beak.

6 Sqeeze the top of the head gently to make a new crease.

7 Repeat the same folding technique with the base of what will form the neck, lifting and squeezing the fold flat.

8 Follow this step carefully as a very small area is being folded. Fold the beak down in a valley fold.

9 Fold the beak up vertically as shown.

10 Finally fold the beak across to the left.

11 Unfold all the creases made in Steps 8-10, open the beak slightly and push the folds inside.

12 Open the wing section at the back of the swan outwards. It is important to keep your folds as sharp as possible when making the tiny head of the swan.

Antelope

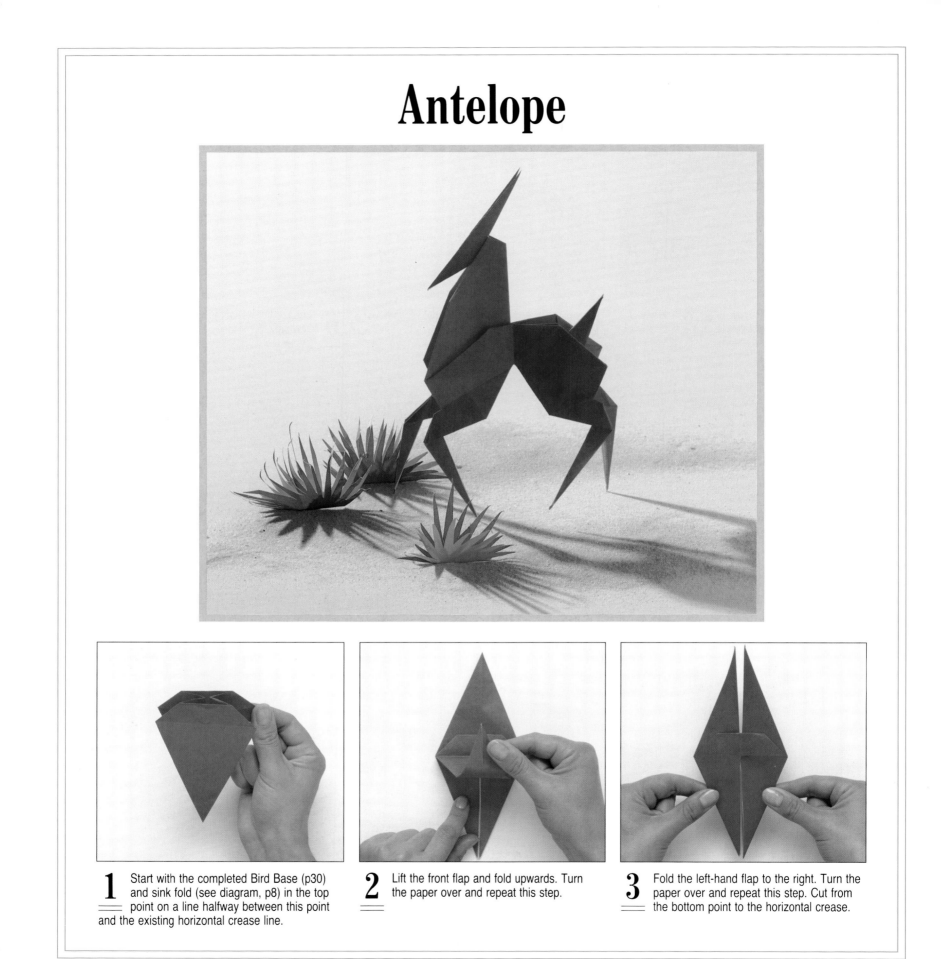

1 Start with the completed Bird Base (p30) and sink fold (see diagram, p8) in the top point on a line halfway between this point and the existing horizontal crease line.

2 Lift the front flap and fold upwards. Turn the paper over and repeat this step.

3 Fold the left-hand flap to the right. Turn the paper over and repeat this step. Cut from the bottom point to the horizontal crease.

4 Fold up the bottom right-hand flap as shown. Turn the shape over and repeat this step.

5 Squash fold the upturned flap carefully. Turn the shape over and repeat this step.

6 Petal fold (see Four or Eight-pointed Star, p21) the flap made in Step 5 as shown. Turn the shape over and repeat this step.

7 Fold the right-hand flap in half, turn the shape over and repeat this step.

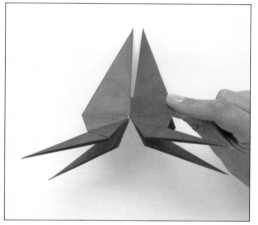

8 Follow Steps 4-7, exactly as before, with the flaps on the other side.

9 Inside reverse fold (see diagram, p8) the four narrow flaps; then inside reverse fold the top right-hand flap down.

10 Fold the small flap on the right-hand side to curve the antelope's torso; then fold the small left-hand edge at the base of the antelope's neck similarly.

11 Inside reverse fold the main part of the tail so that it stands up.

12 Using a craft knife or sharp scissors, make a cut in the top left-hand flap and inside reverse fold this top point to complete the antelope.

Frog

1 Start with the completed frog base (see Iris, p36). Position the base with the open flaps at the bottom.

2 Fold the left-hand flap across to the right, turn the paper over and fold the right-hand flap to the left.

3 Fold the lower edges of the front flaps so that the edges meet in the center. Repeat this step on the other three sides.

4 Return the top right-hand flap to the left, turn the shape over and return the top left-hand flap to the right.

5 Inside reverse fold (see diagram, p8) the front two lower points upwards as far as they will go to form the front legs.

6 Inside reverse fold the other two lower points to the left and right to form the back legs.

7 Inside reverse fold the front legs close to the frog's body.

8 Inside reverse fold the back legs as shown.

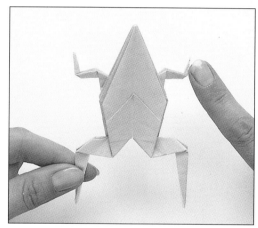

9 Inside reverse fold the tips of the front legs.

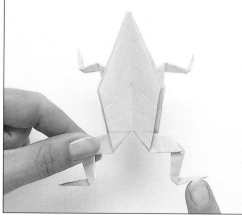

10 Inside reverse fold the tips of the back legs to form the feet.

11 Blow into the hole at the bottom of the frog to inflate it and press down slightly on the top point.

12 Use beads for the eyes. Place on a flat surface; press firmly on the base of the frog's body to make it jump.

Umbrella

1 This is not strictly origami as, in addition to two 10 inch squares of paper, you will also need a thin dowel stick, some tape and a pair of scissors. Fold one square of paper into the Preliminary Base (p30).

2 Position the square as shown. Lift the top layer of the left-hand flap and squash fold; then fold the left-hand side of the fold onto the right. Repeat with the other three flaps, bringing the right-hand ones to the left in turn.

3 The shape now has four flaps on each side.

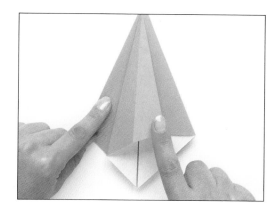  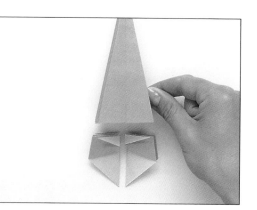

4 Squash fold the left-hand flap and fold the left-hand side of the fold onto the right, as in Step 2. Repeat this step with each of the other seven flaps in turn.

5 The shape now has eight flaps on each side.

6 Cut through all the layers just below the horizontal edge; then cut off a tiny bit of the tip. Repeat Steps 1-5 using the second square of paper.

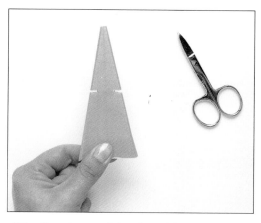  

7 On only one of the pleated forms, measure the halfway mark and using a pair of scissors, cut a small slit through all the layers on both sides. Each slit should be a quarter of the overall width at that point.

8 Holding the tip with one hand, open up the form below the cuts with the other hand and crease the valley folds on the outside into mountain folds.

9 Insert the form made in Step 8 into the second pleated form, holding it in place with a little glue.

10 Thread a piece of thin dowel stick (or you can use a chopstick) very carefully through the umbrella.

11 Secure the top of the umbrella 'frame' to the dowel stick with narrow tape in a suitable color.

12 Wrap a piece of paper around the base of the opening mechanism; only glue one end to the mechanism itself so that the inside of the umbrella can move up and down to open and close.

Scottish Terrier

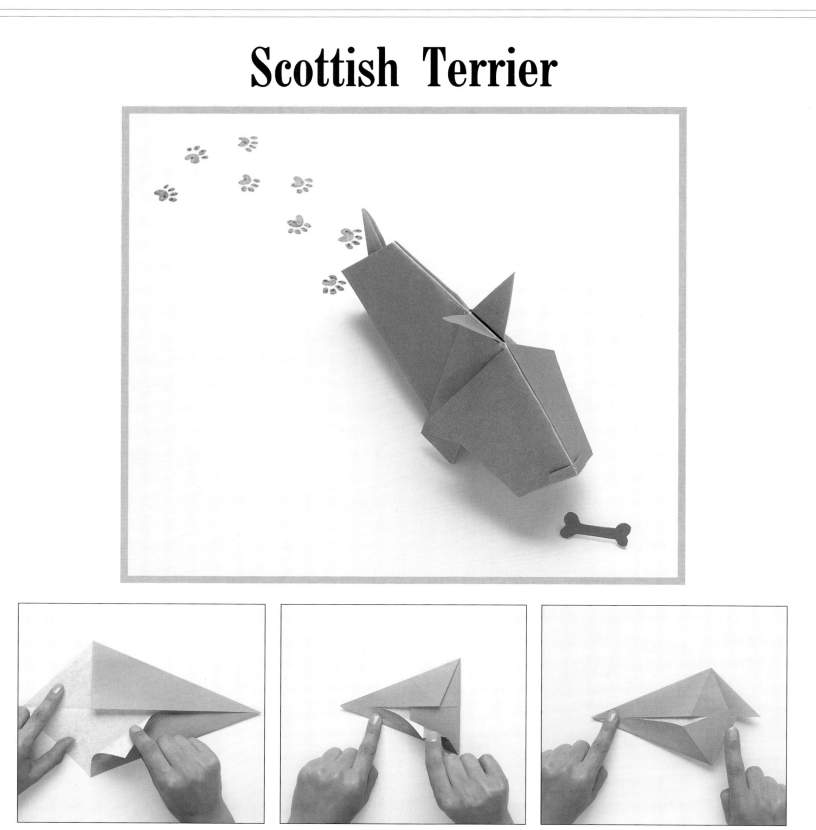

1 Make a diagonal crease in a square of paper; then fold in the two adjacent edges to meet at the center as shown. Gray paper has been used to show the folds more clearly than black.

2 Mountain fold in half so the points meet at the left. Fold in two edges as shown.

3 Pull out the concealed points carefully and flatten them as shown.

4 Bring the lower flap out to the right to form a diamond shape; then fold the central flaps to the left.

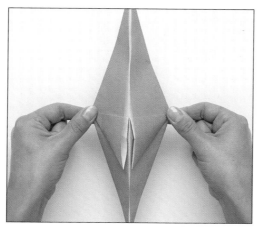

5 Mountain fold the model in half.

6 Hold the point of the central flap and tuck it inside the top layer, leaving a small projecting triangle.

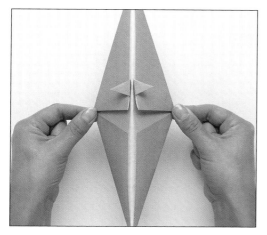

7 Turn the shape over and repeat Step 6 on this side. Fold back both small triangles over the respective sides.

8 Valley fold the top flap over the bottom one on the horizontal line, and fold back to form a pleat in the center. Turn the shape over.

9 Fold down the top point so that it meets the horizontal line.

10 Valley fold the same point back over and over so that it extends just beyond the new horizontal line.

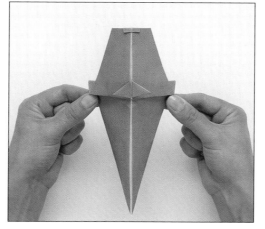

11 Mountain fold the projecting edge and fold the whole model in half as shown.

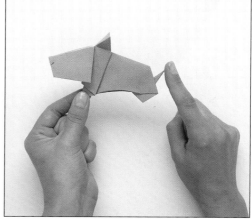

12 Inside reverse fold (see diagram, p8) the long point twice to form the rear legs and tail. Mountain fold the bottom edge of the body slightly; shape the head with a pleat.

Snail

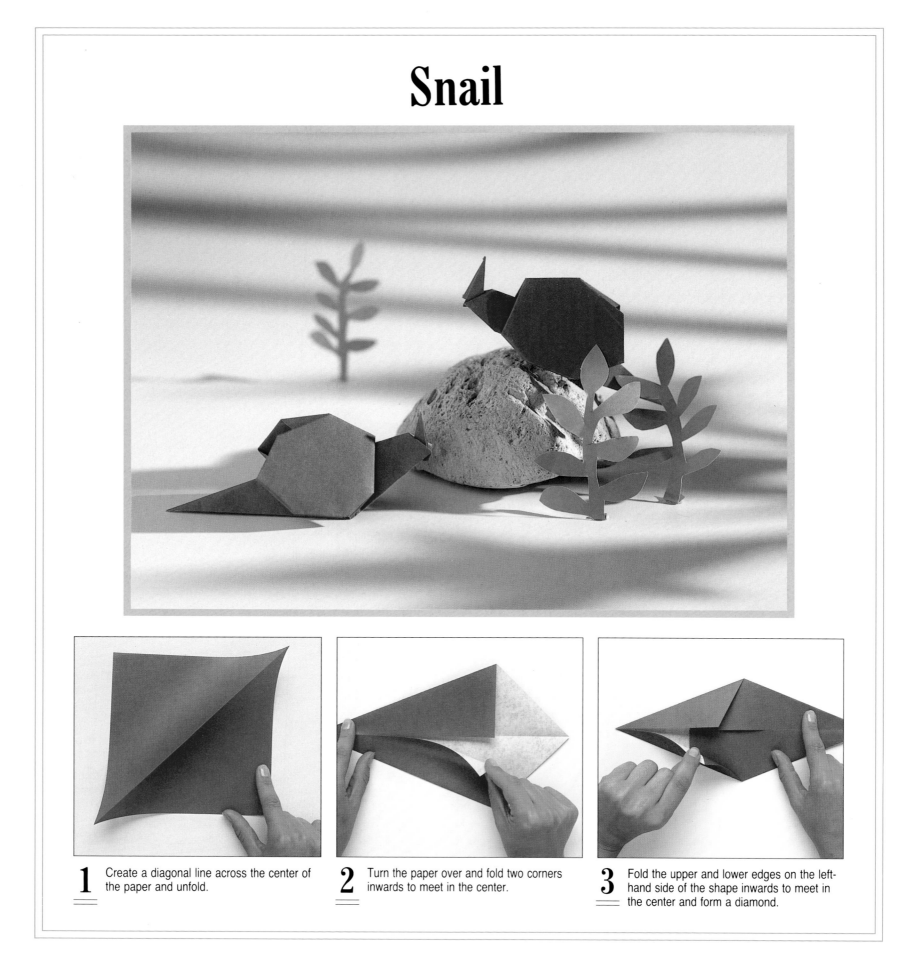

1 Create a diagonal line across the center of the paper and unfold.

2 Turn the paper over and fold two corners inwards to meet in the center.

3 Fold the upper and lower edges on the left-hand side of the shape inwards to meet in the center and form a diamond.

4 Position the diamond as shown and valley fold the bottom point upwards to meet the top point and form a triangle.

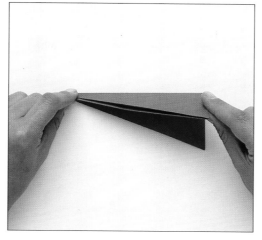

5 Keeping one finger on the apex as shown, bring the top corner over to the bottom to fold the shape in half.

6 Position the shape so that the open angles are on the right.

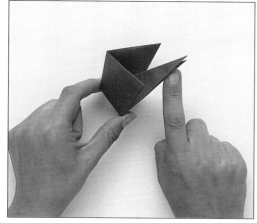

7 Inside reverse fold (see diagram, p8) the left-hand point carefully to extend beyond the two open angles.

8 Inside reverse fold the inner layer of this left-hand point back to its original position, leaving the outer layer.

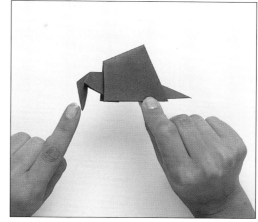

9 Inside reverse fold the top point of the left-hand triangle.

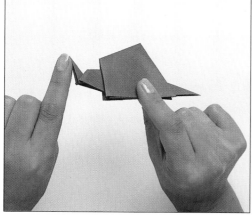

10 Inside reverse fold this point back again to create the head and antennas.

11 Inside reverse fold the top of the snail shell so that the point lies inside.

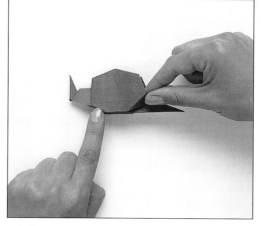

12 Mountain fold the two points of the lower shell so that you make this section appear rounder.

Index

A

Antelope 54

B

Bird Base 31
Booklet 20
Box on Legs 27
Bracelet 34
Butterfly 24

C

Coaster 11
Corner Fastener 22
Crown, the 14
Cubic Gift Box 42
Cup 18
Cygnet 46

F

Flower Decorations 15
Flying Crane 48
Frog 56

G

G I Hat 28
Goldfish 17

I

Iris 36

M

Mouse 50

P

Picture Frame 44
Preliminary Base 30

R

Rooster 38

S

Salt Cellar 12
Samurai Hat 16
Scottish Terrier 60
Seed Envelope 23
Shallow Box 26
Simple Boat 32
Snail 62
Spanish Box 13
Star, Four- or Eight-pointed 21
Star-shaped Box 40
Swan 52

U

Umbrella 58

W

Windmill 10

Y

Yakko-San 19